# THE HISTORY OF FOODS
# DRINKS

by Kristine Spanier, MLIS

pogo

## Ideas for Parents and Teachers

Pogo Books let children practice reading informational text while introducing them to nonfiction features such as headings, labels, sidebars, maps, and diagrams, as well as a table of contents, glossary, and index.

Carefully leveled text with a strong photo match offers early fluent readers the support they need to succeed.

### Before Reading
- "Walk" through the book and point out the various nonfiction features. Ask the student what purpose each feature serves.
- Look at the glossary together. Read and discuss the words.

### During Reading
- Have the child read the book independently.
- Invite them to list questions that arise from reading.

### After Reading
- Discuss the child's questions. Talk about how they might find answers to those questions.
- Prompt the child to think more. Ask: Have you thought about all the choices you have when you're thirsty? How do you decide what to drink?

Pogo Books are published by Jump!
3500 American Blvd W, Suite 150
Bloomington, MN 55431
www.jumplibrary.com

Copyright © 2026 Jump!
International copyright reserved in all countries. No part of this book may be reproduced in any form without written permission from the publisher.

Jump! is a division of FlutterBee Education Group.

Library of Congress Cataloging-in-Publication Data

Names: Spanier, Kristine, author.
Title: Drinks / by Kristine Spanier, MLIS.
Description: Minneapolis, MN: Jump!, Inc., [2026]
Series: The history of foods | Includes index.
Audience: Ages 7–10
Identifiers: LCCN 2025001193 (print)
LCCN 2025001194 (ebook)
ISBN 9798892139090 (hardcover)
ISBN 9798892139106 (paperback)
ISBN 9798892139113 (ebook)
Subjects: LCSH: Beverages—History—Juvenile literature.
Inventors—History—Juvenile literature.
Classification: LCC TX815 .S725 2026 (print)
LCC TX815 (ebook)
DDC 641.209—dc23/eng/20250208
LC record available at https://lccn.loc.gov/2025001193
LC ebook record available at https://lccn.loc.gov/2025001194

Editor: Jenna Gleisner
Designer: Molly Ballanger

Photo Credits: gresei/Shutterstock, cover; tastyfood/Shutterstock, 1; Mehmet Hilmi Barcin/iStock, 3; New Africa/Shutterstock, 4; adsR/Alamy, 5; Nitiphonphat/Shutterstock, 6-7; Jaclyn Vernace/Shutterstock, 8-9; Retro AdArchives/Alamy, 9, 12 (right), 14-15; fcafotodigital/iStock, 10-11; digitalreflections/Shutterstock, 11; James Elliott/Dreamstime, 12 (left); Gabby Jones/Bloomberg/Getty, 13; Steve Cukrov/Shutterstock, 16; David Tonelson/Dreamstime, 17; Jaimie Trueblood/WireImage/Getty, 18-19; Mushiii/Shutterstock, 20-21 (foreground); Michael Siluk/Shutterstock, 20-21 (background); homank76/Adobe Stock, 23.

Printed in the United States of America at Corporate Graphics in North Mankato, Minnesota.

# TABLE OF CONTENTS

**CHAPTER 1**
**Fruits, Syrups, and Powders**..................4

**CHAPTER 2**
**Drinks on the Go**..................12

**CHAPTER 3**
**Selling Water**..................16

**QUICK FACTS & TOOLS**
**Timeline**..................22
**Glossary**..................23
**Index**..................24
**To Learn More**..................24

# CHAPTER 1
# FRUITS, SYRUPS, AND POWDERS

Do you like lemonade? It is made with lemon juice, water, and sugar. The first U.S. **recipe** for this drink is from 1824. It is more than 200 years old!

Another fruit juice became popular in the 1800s. In 1869, Thomas Welch cooked grapes. He bottled the juice to sell later. It was the first **preserved** fruit juice sold in the United States.

CHAPTER 1  5

John Pemberton **invented** a **syrup** in 1886. It had an **ingredient** from coca leaves. It also had **caffeine**. He mixed it with **carbonated** water. It was named Coca-Cola. It was the first soda!

### DID YOU KNOW?

Caleb Bradham wanted to copy Coca-Cola. He made a soda recipe in 1893. First, it was called Brad's Drink. The name changed to Pepsi-Cola in 1898.

In the 1900s, Edwin Perkins created Fruit Smack. In 1927, he removed the liquid from the mix. A powder was left. It could be sold in envelopes. He gave it a new name. It was Kool-Ade! Later, the spelling changed to Kool-Aid.

### WHAT DO YOU THINK?

Kool-Ade first came in six **flavors**. They were grape, lemon-lime, cherry, orange, raspberry, and strawberry. What flavors would you create? Why?

CHAPTER 1

envelope

CHAPTER 1   9

Charles Sanna made powdered creamer. He had too much. He **experimented**. He mixed the powder with cocoa, sugar, and vanilla. Then he added hot water. He named it Swiss Miss cocoa mix. He started selling it in 1961. People could have hot cocoa in an instant!

CHAPTER 1   11

## CHAPTER 2

# DRINKS ON THE GO

Football players in Florida get hot! They need to stay **hydrated**. In 1965, University of Florida scientists worked on a new drink. It had **electrolytes**. They called it Gatorade. Why? It was named after the mascot!

mascot

Rudolf Wild worked in Germany. In 1969, he created a fruit drink. He called it Capri-Sonne. It was in a pouch. It could stand up. The first flavors were lemon and orange. Later, the name changed to Capri-Sun. It came to the United States in 1982.

CHAPTER 2    13

In the late 1900s, the Coca-Cola Company made more kinds of soda. More than 165 million Coke **products** were sold every 24 hours. That is more than 60 billion drinks a year! Today, the company sells more than 1.6 billion drinks each day!

CHAPTER 2

# CHAPTER 3
# SELLING WATER

Water should be free, right? Not always! Perrier is a carbonated spring water. It is from France. In 1977, a new **advertisement** came out. It said the water was a healthy drink.

New **brands** of bottled water came out. By 2016, bottled water was sold more than soda!

CHAPTER 3   17

This led to new water drinks. John Bikoff created Smartwater and Vitaminwater in 1996. These have electrolytes, **vitamins**, and **minerals**.

CHAPTER 3

# TAKE A LOOK!

What were the most popular drinks in the United States in 2023? Take a look!

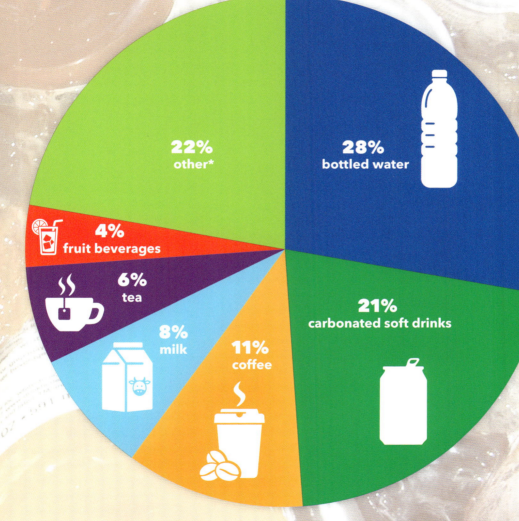

*includes tap water, sports drinks, and adult beverages

CHAPTER 3

CHAPTER 3

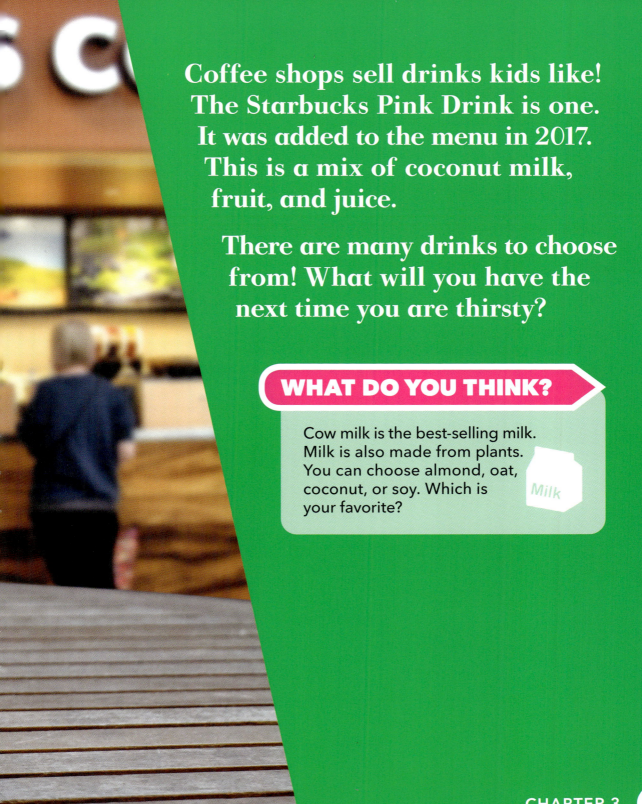

Coffee shops sell drinks kids like! The Starbucks Pink Drink is one. It was added to the menu in 2017. This is a mix of coconut milk, fruit, and juice.

There are many drinks to choose from! What will you have the next time you are thirsty?

### WHAT DO YOU THINK?

Cow milk is the best-selling milk. Milk is also made from plants. You can choose almond, oat, coconut, or soy. Which is your favorite?

CHAPTER 3 — 21

# QUICK FACTS & TOOLS

## TIMELINE

Take a look at some important dates in the history of drinks!

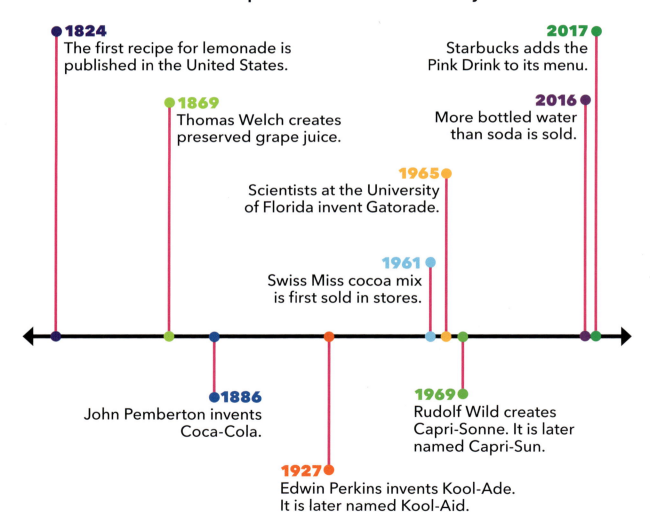

- **1824** The first recipe for lemonade is published in the United States.
- **1869** Thomas Welch creates preserved grape juice.
- **1886** John Pemberton invents Coca-Cola.
- **1927** Edwin Perkins invents Kool-Ade. It is later named Kool-Aid.
- **1961** Swiss Miss cocoa mix is first sold in stores.
- **1965** Scientists at the University of Florida invent Gatorade.
- **1969** Rudolf Wild creates Capri-Sonne. It is later named Capri-Sun.
- **2016** More bottled water than soda is sold.
- **2017** Starbucks adds the Pink Drink to its menu.

# GLOSSARY

**advertisement:** A commercial, poster, or other method that shows or tells people about a product or service so that people want to buy or use it.

**brands:** Names that identify a product or the company that makes it.

**caffeine:** A chemical found in tea, coffee, and some soft drinks that prompts activity in the body.

**carbonated:** Having fizz or bubbles because it contains carbon dioxide gas.

**electrolytes:** Minerals the human body needs to function.

**experimented:** Tested or tried something in order to learn something particular.

**flavors:** Tastes.

**hydrated:** Having enough liquid so one's body feels good and works well.

**ingredient:** An item used to make something.

**invented:** Created and produced for the first time.

**minerals:** Solid substances found in the earth that the human body needs to function.

**preserved:** Treated so that it does not spoil.

**products:** Items that are made, grown, or created to be sold or used by people.

**recipe:** Instructions for preparing a food or drink, including what ingredients are needed.

**syrup:** A thick, sweet liquid made by boiling sugar and water, usually with flavoring.

**vitamins:** Substances in food that are essential for good health and nutrition.

QUICK FACTS & TOOLS

# INDEX

Bikoff, John 18
bottled water 17, 19
Bradham, Caleb 7
caffeine 7
Capri-Sun 13
Coca-Cola 7
Coca-Cola Company 15
fruit juice 4, 5, 21
Gatorade 12
Kool-Aid 8
lemonade 4
milk 19, 21
Pemberton, John 7
Pepsi-Cola 7
Perkins, Edwin 8
Perrier 16
powder 8, 11
Sanna, Charles 11
Smartwater 18
Starbucks 21
Swiss Miss 11
Vitaminwater 18
Welch, Thomas 5
Wild, Rudolf 13

# TO LEARN MORE

**Finding more information is as easy as 1, 2, 3.**

❶ Go to www.factsurfer.com
❷ Enter "drinks" into the search box.
❸ Choose your book to see a list of websites.